Jan. 2013

Dear Knute and Pennie,
    Like "one bird singing back
to another because it
can't not," this book
will surely sing to you.
        Much love,
            Jillisa Hope Milner

COME, THIEF

COME, THIEF

POEMS

Jane Hirshfield

Alfred A. Knopf · New York · 2011

THIS IS A BORZOI BOOK
PUBLISHED BY ALFRED A. KNOPF

Knopf, Borzoi Books, and the colophon are
registered trademarks of Random House, Inc.

Library of Congress Cataloging-in-Publication Data

Hirshfield, Jane, 1953–
Come, thief : poems / by Jane Hirshfield. — 1st ed.
p.   cm.
"A Borzoi Book."
ISBN 978-0-307-59542-3
I. Title.
PS3558.I694C66 2011
811'.54—dc22   2010051493

Jacket photograph by Lane Coder / GalleryStock

Jacket design by Barbara de Wilde

Manufactured in the United States of America
Published August 25, 2011
Second Printing, September 2011

for Carl

CONTENTS

COME, THIEF

FRENCH HORN

For a few days only,
the plum tree outside the window
shoulders perfection.
No matter the plums will be small,
eaten only by squirrels and jays.
I feast on the one thing, they on another,
the shoaling bees on a third.
What in this unpleated world isn't someone's seduction?
The boy playing his intricate horn in Mahler's Fifth,
in the gaps between playing,
turns it and turns it, dismantles a section,
shakes from it the condensation
of human passage. He is perhaps twenty.
Later he takes his four bows, his face deepening red,
while a girl holds a viola's spruce wood and maple
in one half-opened hand and looks at him hard.
Let others clap.
These two, their ears still ringing, hear nothing.
Not the shouts of *bravo, bravo,*
not the timpanic clamor inside their bodies.
As the plum's blossoms do not hear the bee
nor taste themselves turned into storable honey
by that sumptuous disturbance.

FIRST LIGHT EDGING CIRRUS

10^{25} molecules
are enough
to call wood thrush or apple.

A hummingbird, fewer.
A wristwatch: 10^{24}.

An alphabet's molecules,
tasting of honey, iron, and salt,
cannot be counted—

as some strings, untouched,
sound when a near one is speaking.

So it was when love slipped inside us.
It looked out face to face in every direction.

Then it was inside the tree, the rock, the cloud.

THE DECISION

There is a moment before a shape
hardens, a color sets.
Before the fixative or heat of kiln.
The letter might still be taken
from the mailbox.
The hand held back by the elbow,
the word kept between the larynx pulse
and the amplifying drum-skin of the room's air.
The thorax of an ant is not as narrow.
The green coat on old copper weighs more.
Yet something slips through it—
looks around,
sets out in the new direction, for other lands.
Not into exile, not into hope. Simply changed.
As a sandy track-rut changes when called a Silk Road:
it cannot be after turned back from.

Vinegar and Oil

Wrong solitude vinegars the soul,
right solitude oils it.

How fragile we are, between the few good moments.

Coming and going unfinished,
puzzled by fate,

like the half-carved relief
of a fallen donkey, above a church door in Finland.

THE TONGUE SAYS LONELINESS

The tongue says loneliness, anger, grief,
but does not feel them.

As Monday cannot feel Tuesday,
nor Thursday
reach back to Wednesday
as a mother reaches out for her found child.

As this life is not a gate, but the horse plunging through it.

Not a bell,
but the sound of the bell in the bell-shape,
lashing full strength with the first blow from inside the iron.

Big-Leaf Maple Standing over Its Own Reflection

For a dog,
no news the wind brings is without interest.
A boat's hull does not travel last year's waves.

A lit window at night in the distance:
idea almost graspable, finally not.

"How many feet of skim milk does it take
to shingle a lamppost?"
my friend's teacher would ask him.
"Lightning, like luck, lands somewhere,"
my friend would reply.

The feeling heart does not tire of carrying ballast.

The members of one Siberian tribe
spoke of good things in metaphor only:

"The gods are jealous, but stupid," they kindly explained.

A lake-water's listing, this knowledge.
Small winds disturbed the leaves of a nearby maple,
then turned them away—
whether toward suffering or from it, harder to say.

CRITIQUE OF PURE REASON

"Like one man milking a billy goat,
another holding a sieve beneath it,"
Kant wrote, quoting an unnamed ancient.
It takes a moment to notice the sieve doesn't matter.
In her nineties, a woman begins to sleepwalk.
One morning finding pudding and a washed pot,
another the opened drawers of her late husband's dresser.
After a while, anything becomes familiar,
though the Yiddish jokes of Auschwitz
stumbled and failed outside the barbed wire.
Perimeter is not meaning, but it changes meaning,
as wit increases distance and compassion erodes it.
Let reason flow like water around a stone, the stone remains.
A dog catching a tennis ball lobbed into darkness
holds her breath silent, to keep the descent in her ears.
The goat stands patient for two millennia,
watching without judgment from behind his strange eyes.

NARROWNESS

Day after day,
my neighbors' cats in the garden.

Each in a distant spot,
like wary planets.

One brindled gray,
one black and white,
one orange.

They remind of the feelings:
how one cannot know another completely.

The way two cats cannot sleep
in one patch of mint-scented shade.

These Also Once under Moonlight

A snake
with two small hind-limbs
and pelvic girdle.

Large-headed dinosaurs
hunting in packs like dogs.
Others whose scaly plates
thistle to feathers.

Mammals sleekening, ottering,
simplified
back toward the waters.

Ours, too, a transitional species,
chimerical, passing,
what is later, always, called monstrous—
no longer one thing, not yet another.

Fossils greeting fossils,
fearful, hopeful.
Walking, sleeping, waking, wanting to live.

Nuzzling our young wildly, as they did.

"DISTANCE MAKES CLEAN"

Best when the gods changed
into rag and sandal,
thinness, wrinkle,
knocked, asked entrance.

Such test is simple, can be passed or failed:
The softest bed.
The meat unstinting.

But when from far and mountain
they would ask,
and for amusement, "What are mortals?"
even the flocking creatures came to tremble, cattle, sheep.

Scentless   silent
then
the distant slaughters, like toy armies in the hands of boys.

Of Yield and Abandon

A muscular, thick-pelted woodchuck,
created in yield, in abandon, lifts onto his haunches.
Behind him, abundance of ferns, a rock wall's
coldness, never in sun, a few noisy grackles.
Our eyes find shining beautiful
because it reminds us of water. To say this
does not make fewer the rooms of the house
or lessen its zinc-ceilinged hallways.
There is something that waits inside us,
a nearness that fissures, that fishes. Leaf shine
and stone shine edging the tail of the woodchuck silver,
splashing the legs of chickens and clouds.
In Russian, the translator told me,
there is no word for "thirsty"—a sentence,
as always, impossible to translate.
But what is the point of preserving the bell
if to do so it must be filled with concrete or wax?
A body prepared for travel but not for singing.

The Conversation

A woman moves close:
there is something she wants to say.
The currents take you one direction, her another.
All night you are aware of her presence,
aware of the conversation that did not happen.
Inside it are mountains, birds, a wide river,
a few sparse-leaved trees.
On the river, a wooden boat putters.
On its deck, a spider washes its face.
Years from now, the boat will reach a port by the sea,
and the generations of spider descendants upon it
will look out, from their nearsighted, eightfold eyes,
at something unanswered.

PERISHABLE, IT SAID

Perishable, it said on the plastic container,
and below, in different ink,
the date to be used by, the last teaspoon consumed.

I found myself looking:
now at the back of each hand,
now inside the knees,
now turning over each foot to look at the sole.

Then at the leaves of the young tomato plants,
then at the arguing jays.

Under the wooden table and lifted stones, looking.
Coffee cups, olives, cheeses,
hunger, sorrow, fears—
these too would certainly vanish, without knowing when.

How suddenly then
the strange happiness took me,
like a man with strong hands and strong mouth,
inside that hour with its perishing perfumes and clashings.

Fourth World

A friend dies.
A horse dies.
A man dies over and over again on the news.

Without them,
the fourth world continues.
Waking fox-red on the flanks of the mountain.

Absence, anger, grief,
cruelty, failure—
The fox walks through them.

It wants, as she had, to live.

All day it is cool in the shadows, hot in the sun.

BRUISES

In age, the world grows clumsy.

A heavy jar
leaps from a cupboard.
A suitcase has corners.

Others have no explanation.

Old love, old body,
do you remember—
carpet burns down the spine,
gravel bedding
the knees, hardness to hardness.

You who knew yourself
kissed by the bite of the ant,
you who were kissed by the bite of the spider.

Now kissed by this.

The Pear

November. One pear
sways on the tree past leaves, past reason.
In the nursing home, my friend has fallen.
Chased, he said, from the freckled woods
by angry Thoreau, Coleridge, and Beaumarchais.
Delusion too, it seems, can be well-read.
He is courteous, well-spoken even in dread.
The old fineness in him hangs on
for dear life. "My mind now?
A small ship under the wake of a large.
They force you to walk on your heels here,
the angles matter. Four or five degrees,
and you're lost." Life is dear to him yet,
though he believes it his own fault he grieves,
his own fault his old friends have turned against him
like crows against an injured of their kind.
There is no kindness here, no flint of mercy.
Descend, descend,
some voice must urge, inside the pear-stem.
The argument goes on, he cannot outrun it.
Dawnlight to dawnlight, I look: it is still there.

ALZHEIMER'S

When a fine old carpet
is eaten by mice,
the colors and patterns
of what's left behind
do not change.
As bedrock, tilted,
stays bedrock,
its purple and red striations unbroken.
Unstrippable birthright grandeur.
"How are you," I asked,
not knowing what to expect.
"Contrary to Keatsian joy," he replied.

Heat and Desperation

Preparation, she thought,
as if a pianist,
limbering, stretching.
But fingers are tendon, not spirit;
are bone and muscle and skin.
Increase of reach extends reach,
but not what comes then to fill it.
What comes to fill it is something that has no name,
a hunger from outside the wolf-colored edges.
Thirteen smoke jumpers died at Mann Gulch.
Two ran faster.
One stopped, set a match ahead of himself,
ahead of the fire. Then stepped upslope,
lay down inside still-burning ashes, and lived.

Left-Handed Sugar

In nature, molecules are chiral—they turn in one direction or the other. Naturally then, someone wondered: might sugar, built to mirror itself, be sweet, but pass through the body unnoticed? A dieter's gold mine. I don't know why the experiment failed, or how. I think of the loneliness of that man-made substance, like a ghost in a '50s movie you could pass your hand through, or some suitor always rejected despite the sparkle of his cubic zirconia ring. Yet this sugar is real, and somewhere exists. It looks for a left-handed tongue.

The Promise

Stay, I said
to the cut flowers.
They bowed
their heads lower.

Stay, I said to the spider,
who fled.

Stay, leaf.
It reddened,
embarrassed for me and itself.

Stay, I said to my body.
It sat as a dog does,
obedient for a moment,
soon starting to tremble.

Stay, to the earth
of riverine valley meadows,
of fossiled escarpments,
of limestone and sandstone.
It looked back
with a changing expression, in silence.

Stay, I said to my loves.
Each answered,
Always.

RED WINE IS FINED BY
ADDING BROKEN EGGSHELLS

Red wine is fined by adding broken
eggshells or bull's blood,
but does not taste of the animal traveled through it.

Cold leather of fog on the day, then only the day,
cleared and simple,
whose windows lift equally into what light happens.

The dog asks to go out and you let her,
age rough in her coat as stairs that keep no landing.

The familiar is not safety.

Yet a horse unblindered runs back to the shape it knows burning.

THE LOST LOVE POEMS OF SAPPHO

The poems we haven't read
must be her fiercest:
imperfect, extreme.
As it is with love, its nights, its days.
It stands on the top of the mountain
and looks for more mountain, steeper pitches.
Descent a thought impossible to imagine.

Building and Earthquake

How easy it is for a dream to construct
both building and earthquake.
Also the nine flights of wooden stairs in the dark,
and the trembling horse, its hard breathing
loud in the sudden after-silence and starlight.
This time the dream allows the building to stand.
Something it takes the dreamer a long time to notice,
who thought that the fear was the meaning
when being able to feel the fear was the meaning.

Each We Call Fate

What some could not have escaped
others will find by decision.

Each we call fate. Which Forgetfulness—
sister of Memory—will take back.
Not distinguishing necessity from choice,
not weighing courage against betrayal or luck.

"Did you then have your life?" the black crows will ask.

"Scent of strong tea," you may answer.
"Color of swimming tuna, seen from below.
Grounds of the palace illimitable with mice and rabbits."

The Visible Heat

Near even a candle, the visible heat.
So it is with a person in love:
buying bread, paying a bridge toll.
You too have been that woman,
the one who is looked at and the one who looks.
Each lowers the eyes before it, without knowing why.

Sometimes the Heart Is a Shallow Autumn River

Is rock and shadow, bird.
Is fry, as the smallest fish are called,
darting in the pan of nearness.

The frog's flawless interpretation of the music "Leaf"
is a floating black-eyed emerald
slipped between the water and its reflections.

And caution, and hope, and sorrow?
As umbrellas are, to a mountain or field of grass.

Love in August

White moths
against the screen
in August darkness.

Some clamor
in envy.

Some spread large
as two hands
of a thief

who wants to put
back in your cupboard
the long-taken silver.

Two Rains

The dog came in
and shook off
water in every direction.

A chaotic rainstorm,
walking on four big paws.

The outside rain
fell straight,
in parallel lines
from a child's drawing.

Windless, blunt, and cold,
that orderly rain,
like a fate
uninterrupted by late love.

Washing Doorknobs

The glass doorknobs turn no differently.
But every December
I polish them with vinegar water and cotton.

Another year ends.
This one, I ate Kyoto pickles
and touched, in Xi'an, a stone turtle's face,
cold as stone, as turtle.

I could not read the fortune carved into its shell
or hear what it had raised its head
to listen for, such a long time.

Around it, the madness of empires continued,
an unbitted horse that runs for a thousand miles
between grazing.

Around us, the madness of empires continues.

How happy we are,
how unhappy we are, doesn't matter.
The stone turtle listens. The famished horse runs.

Washing doorknobs, one year enters another.

CHAPEL

The moonlight builds its cold chapel
again out of piecemeal darkness.
You who have ears and hands, it says, *come in;*
no need to stamp the snow-weight from your shoes.
It lifts another block and begins to chisel:
Kyoto, Vladivostok, Chicago, Beijing, Perth.
Huge-handed, working around you in silence,
as a cat will enter the silence where no dog lives.

TOLSTOY AND THE SPIDER

Moscow is burning.
Pierre sets out to kill Napoléon
and instead rescues a child.
Thus Tolstoy came today
to lift this spider in his large hand
and carry her free.
Now a cricket approaches the spider
set down inside her new story,
one hind leg missing.
The insects touch, a decision is made,
each moves away from the other
as if two exhausted and unprovisioned armies,
as if two planets passing out of conjunction,
or two royal courts in procession,
neither willing to note the other's passage.
Or like my own two legs:
their narrow lifetime of coming together and parting.
A story travels in one direction only,
no matter how often
it tries to turn north, south, east, west, back.

For the *Lobaria, Usnea,* Witches Hair, Map Lichen, Beard Lichen, Ground Lichen, Shield Lichen

Back then, what did I know?
The names of subway lines, busses.
How long it took to walk twenty blocks.

Uptown and downtown.
Not north, not south, not you.

When I saw you, later, seaweed reefed in the air,
you were gray-green, incomprehensible, old.
What you clung to, hung from: old.
Trees looking half-dead, stones.

Marriage of fungi and algae,
chemists of air,
changers of nitrogen-unusable into nitrogen-usable.

Like those nameless ones
who kept painting, shaping, engraving
unseen, unread, unremembered.
Not caring if they were no good, if they were past it.

Rock wools, water fans, earth scale, mouse ears, dust,
ash-of-the-woods.
Transformers unvalued, uncounted.
Cell by cell, word by word, making a world they could live in.

SWEATER

What is asked of one is not what is asked of another.
A sweater takes on the shape of its wearer,
a coffee cup sits to the left or the right of the workspace,
making its pale Saturn rings of now and before.
Lucky the one who rises to sit at a table,
day after day spilling coffee sweet with sugar, whitened with milk.
Lucky the one who writes in a book of spiral-bound mornings
a future in ink, who writes hand unshaking, warmed by thick wool.
Lucky still, the one who writes later, shaking. Acrobatic at last, the
    sweater,
elastic as breath that enters what shape it is asked to.
Patient the table; unjudging, the ample, refillable cup.
Irrefusable, the shape the sweater is given,
stretched in the shoulders, sleeves lengthened by unmetaphysical
    pullings on.

Seawater Stiffens Cloth

Seawater stiffens cloth long after it's dried.
As pain after it's ended stays in the body:
A woman moves her hands oddly
because her grandfather passed through
a place he never spoke of. Making
instead the old jokes with angled fingers.
Call one thing another's name long enough,
it will answer. Call pain seawater, tree, it will answer.
Call it a tree whose shape of branches happened.
Call what branching happened a man
whose job it was to break fingers or lose his own.
Call fingers angled like branches what peel and cut apples,
to give to a girl who eats them in silence, looking.
Call her afterward tree, call her seawater angled by silence.

The Inventive, Visible Hobbles

The inventive, visible hobbles,
the cigarette, the battery,
the board.

What is done
is done through the body.
What can be stopped
is stopped with the body.

Yet an innocent elbow and fist,
ankle and foot,
touch the innocent shoulders and spine,
anus and breasts of others.

An innocent tongue,
licking innocent air as it speaks,
gives orders to hands
that could be slipping the skin from a peach.

Loud beyond hearing,
a hell where physical flames
might interrogate an apprehendable spirit,
its thighbone and cheekbone.

But no.
The crime goes free.
It dies with the dictator's head on a downy pillow.

"Haofon Rece Swealg"

Batteries,
yellow trucks hauling garbage,
ampicillin, napalm.

These too will be
replaced by the not-yet-imagined.

The engines of diesel
will silence,
joining the engines of steam,
the brayings of mule.

And still the poetry of ancient Sumeria
will be understood with ease—

humiliation,
ambition,
slaughter,
the cutting down of the tallest cedar—

and *Beowulf*'s verdict yet hold:

Technologies alter.

Heaven swallows the smoke.

Shadow: An Assay

Mostly we do not think of, even see you,
shadow,
for your powers at first seem few.

Why command "Heel," ask "Sit,"
when before the thought is conceived,
you are already there?

True that sometimes you run ahead, sometimes behind,
that *early* and *late,*
to you, must be words of the deepest poignance:
while inside them, you are larger than you were.

Midday drives you to reticence, sulking,
a silence
I've felt many times inside me as well.

You came with me to Kraków, Glasgow, Corfu.
Did you enjoy them?
                    I never asked.
Though however close my hand came to the table,
you were closer, touching before my tongue
the herring and cheeses, the turpentine-scented retsina.

Many times I have seen you sacrifice yourself
without hesitation,
disentangling yourself like Anna Karenina from her purse
before passing under the train wheels of her own thoughts.
Like art, though, you are resilient: you rose again.

Are you then afterlife, clutterless premonition?
You shake your head as soon as I do—
no, we think not.
Whatever earth I will vanish silently into, you also will join.

You carry, I have read,
my rages, fears, and self-regard.
You carry, I have read, my unrevealed longings,
and the monster dreamed as a child, tongueless and armless.
Your ordinary loneliness I recognize too as my own.

When you do not exist,
I have gone with you into darkness,

as the self of a former life
goes into the self that was tortured and beaten
and does not emerge again as it was,
though given a clean shirt to leave in, given pants and new shoes.

For this too is shadow, and mine,
however unspoken:
though you are tongueless, and armless, you harm.
Your inaction my own deepest failure, close by my side.

You who take nothing, give nothing, instruct me,
that my fate may weigh more than yours—

The hour is furious, late.
Your reach, horizontal, distant, leans almost forgiving,
almost indistinguishable from what it crosses.

The Question

I tried to ask my dead—
they answered as always.
I tried to ask the black resourceful ants.

The redwoods swayed
in the honeys of branch-light.
The moored boats shuffled their hulls.

Across the water, the city's windows glittered,
a fastness.
The gelding's breath passed over and out of my hand.

And so I came to turn again to you,
my mineral sadness.
To look you eye to open eye. To wait.

All Day the Difficult Waiting

All day the difficult waiting.
"Continuance" repeating itself inside the ears,
as if a verb, or choice.

As if Levin during his long spring in *Anna Karenina*—
reading and suffering
because he could not understand what he read or suffered.

Planting and mowing what was outside him.

The heart's actions
are neither the sentence nor its reprieve.

Salt hay and thistles, above the cold granite.
One bird singing back to another because it can't not.

WILD PLUM

A gray squirrel tests each plum with his nose,
moving from one to another
until he feasts.

It is like watching the ego,
moving from story to story.

A man is proud of his strong brown teeth,
though all his children have died.

This tree the one he was given,
its small, sustaining fruit, some green, some yellow.

Pits drop to the ground,
a little moistness clings in the scorings.

The left-behind branches
winch themselves silently upward,
as if released from long thought.

SHEEP

It is the work of feeling
to undo expectation.

A black-faced sheep
looks back at you as you pass
and your heart is startled
as if by the shadow
of someone once loved.

Neither comforted by this
nor made lonely.

Only remembering
that a self in exile is still a self,
as a bell unstruck for years
is still a bell.

The Dark Hour

The dark hour came
in the night and purred by my ear.
Outside, in rain,
the plush of the mosses stood higher.
Hour without end, without measure.
It opens the window and calls its own name in.

EVERYTHING HAS TWO ENDINGS

Everything has two endings—
a horse, a piece of string, a phone call.

Before a life, air.
And after.

As silence is not silence, but a limit of hearing.

PROTRACTOR

A window is only a window when stepped away from.

To swim in deep water should feel no different from shallow,
and yet it does.

Losses are so. Split into yellows and blues.

A child's protractor proves it:
what begins near quickly grows far, once the lines are allowed to.

As two are in a room, then only one.

Death on one side of the clear glass,
not-death on the other.
Neither saying a word from inside the enlarging.

THE PRESENT

I wanted to give you something—
no stone, clay, bracelet,
no edible leaf could pass through.
Even a molecule's fragrance by then too large.
Giving had been taken, as you soon would be.
Still, I offered the puffs of air shaped to meaning.
They remained air.
I offered memory on memory,
but what is memory that dies with the fallible inks?
I offered apology, sorrow, longing. I offered anger.
How fine is the mesh of death. You can almost see through it.
I stood on one side of the present, you stood on the other.

It Must Be Leaves

Too slow for rain,
too large for tears,
and grief
cannot be seen.
It must be leaves.
But broken
ones, and brown,
not green.

HAIBUN: A MOUNTAIN ROWBOAT

Go for a walk on the mountain. The trail, up many wooden stairs, passes some houses. In front of one, an old man is building a boat. All summer I have watched this mountain rowboat. Like a horse in its stall, patiently waiting for evening hay, it rests on its wooden cradle. Finally, today, it is being painted: a clear Baltic blue. Horses dream. You can see this move through their ears. But the hopes of an old man spill, as waking life does, through the hands.

> amid summer trees
> blue boat high on a mountain
> its paint scent drying

Green-Striped Melons

They lie
under stars in a field.
They lie under rain in a field.
Under sun.

Some people
are like this as well—
like a painting
hidden beneath another painting.

An unexpected weight
the sign of their ripeness.

CHINA

Whales follow
the whale-roads.
Geese,
roads of magnetized air.

To go great distance,
exactitudes matter.

Yet how often
the heart
that set out for Peru
arrives in China,

Steering hard.
Consulting the charts
the whole journey.

COME, THIEF

The mandarin silence of windows before their view,
like guards who nod to every visitor,
"Pass."

"Come, thief,"
the path to the doorway agrees.

A fire requires its own conflagration.
As birth does. As love does.
Saying to time to the end, "Dear one, enter."

SENTENCINGS

A thing too perfect to be remembered:
stone beautiful only when wet.

§

Blinded by light or black cloth—
so many ways
not to see others suffer.

§

Too much longing:

it separates us
like scent from bread,
rust from iron.

§

From very far or very close—
the most resolute folds of the mountain are gentle.

§

As if putting arms into woolen coat sleeves,
we listen to the murmuring dead.

§

Any point of a circle is its start:
desire forgoing fulfillment to go on desiring.

§

In a room in which nothing
has happened,
sweet-scented tobacco.

§

The very old, hands curling into themselves, remember their parents.

§

Think assailable thoughts, or be lonely.

IF TRUTH IS THE LURE, HUMANS ARE FISHES

Under each station of the real,
another glimmers.
And so the love of false-bottomed drawers
and the salt mines outside Kraków,
going down and down without drowning.
A man harms his wife, his child.
He says, "Here is the reason."
She says, "Here is the reason."
The child says nothing,
watching him led away.
If truth is the lure, humans are fishes.
All the fine bones of that eaten-up story,
think about them.
Their salt-cod whiteness on whiteness.

Izmir

Waking
after long travels

not recognizing the light

the windows

the calls of the birds of this place

not even your own planted roses

not knowing if this
is exhaustion
or failure

or transformation into
some changed existence
as yet
unacknowledged

like the fields
of red
and blue tulips
of stylized Izmir

painted now onto a bowl
now onto a vase

A BLESSING FOR WEDDING

Today when persimmons ripen
Today when fox-kits come out of their den into snow
Today when the spotted egg releases its wren song
Today when the maple sets down its red leaves
Today when windows keep their promise to open
Today when fire keeps its promise to warm
Today when someone you love has died
     or someone you never met has died
Today when someone you love has been born
     or someone you will not meet has been born
Today when rain leaps to the waiting of roots in their dryness
Today when starlight bends to the roofs of the hungry and tired
Today when someone sits long inside his last sorrow
Today when someone steps into the heat of her first embrace
Today, let day and dark bless you
With binding of seed and rind bless you
With snow-chill and lavender bless you
Let the vow of this day keep itself wildly and wholly
Spoken and silent, surprise you inside your ears
Sleeping and waking, unfold itself inside your eyes
Let its fierceness and tenderness hold you
Let its vastness be undisguised in all your days

Fifteen Pebbles

Like Moonlight Seen in a Well

Like moonlight seen in a well.

The one who sees it
blocks it.

Hunger

A red horse crops grass.
A black crow
delves bugs from a dirt pile.
A woman watches in envy what is so simple.

Mountain and Mouse

Both move.
One only more slowly.

The Same Words

Come from each mouth
differently.

The Familiar Stairs

How confidently
the blind
descend familiar stairs.

Only those
with something
to lose
grow timid at darkfall.

Rainstorm Visibly Shining in the Left-Out Spoon of a Leaf

Like grief
in certain people's lives:
as if something
still depended on the straightness of the spine.

Glass

Transparent as glass,
the face of the child telling her story.
But how else learn the real,
if not by inventing what might lie outside it?

Paint

What we see is the paint.
Yet somehow the mind
knows the wall,
as the living know death.

A History

Someone first thought it:
an ox gelded, tamed, harnessed to plow.

Then someone realized the wooden yoke could hold two.

After that, mere power of multiplication.
Railroads, airplanes, factory ships canning salmon.

Memorial

When hearing went, you spoke more.
A kindness.

Now I must.

The Cloudy Vase

Past time,
I threw the flowers out,
washed out
the cloudy vase.

How easily
the old clearness
leapt,
like a practiced tiger,
back inside it.

The Perfection of Loss

Like a native speaker
returned
after long exile,
quiet now in two tongues.

Night and Day

Who am I is the question of owls.
Crow says, *Get up.*

Sonoma Fire

Large moon the deep orange of embers.
Also the scent.
The griefs of others—beautiful, at a distance.

Opening the Hands between Here and Here

On the dark road, only the weight of the rope.
Yet the horse is there.

THE KIND MAN

I sold my grandfather's watch,
its rosy gold and stippled pattern
to be melted.
Movement unreparable.
Lid missing.
Chain—there must have been one–
missing.
Its numbers painted
with a single, expert bristle.
I touched the winding stem,
before I passed it over the counter.
The kind man took it,
what I'd brought him as if to the Stasi.
He weighed the honey of time.

ALL THE DIFFICULT HOURS AND MINUTES

All the difficult hours and minutes
are like salted plums in a jar.
Wrinkled, turned steeply into themselves,
they mutter something the color of shark fins to the glass.
Just so, calamity turns toward calmness.
First a jar holds the *umeboshi*, then the rice does.

Rain Thinking

When it is finally quiet—
the loud refrigerator
still at the same time the heat is—
I hear the sound
and awaken.
Like a cat cleaning herself in the night,
or a dog opening
and closing his mouth
the way they do at times
when thinking,
as if tasting something new.

INVITATION

An invitation arrives
in the morning mail.

Before you have said yes or no,
your arms
slip into its coat sleeves,

and on your feet,
the only shoes bearable
for many days' travel.

Unseen, the two small fawns
grazing in sun outside the window,
their freckled haunches
and hooves' black teaspoons.

Abandoned, the ripening zucchini inside the fence.

Kraków, Galway, Beijing—
how is a city folded so lightly
inside a half-ounce envelope and some ink?

That small museum outside Philadephia,
is it still open,
and if so, is there a later train?

The moment averts its eyes from this impoliteness.

It waits for its guest
to return to her bathrobe and slippers,
her cup of good coffee, her manners.

The morning paper,
rustling in hand,
gives off a present fragrance, however slight.

But invitation's perfume?—
Quick as a kidnap,
faithless as adultery,
fatal as hope.

CONTENTMENT

I had lived on this earth
more than fifty years
before hearing the sound
of sixteen New Hampshire Reds
settling in before sleep.
Dusk gathered
like a handkerchief
into a pouch
of clean straw.
But only fifteen
adjusted themselves
on the wooden couch.
One, with more white in her feathers
than the feathers of others,
still wandered outside,
away from the chuckling,
some quiet joke
neither she nor I quite heard.
"The foxes will have you," I told her.
She scratched the ground,
found a late insect to feast on,
set her clipped beak to peck at my shoe.
Reached for, she ran.
Ran from the ramp
I herded her toward as well.
I tried *raccoons,* then *cold.*
I tried *stew.*
She found a fresh seed.

Her legs were white and clean
and appeared very strong.
We ran around the coop
that way a long time,
she seeming delighted, I flapping.
Darkness, not I, brought her in.

The Egg Had Frozen, an Accident.
I Thought of My Life

The egg had frozen, an accident.
I thought of my life.
I heated the butter anyhow.
The shell peeled easily,
inside it looked
both translucent and boiled.
I moved it around in the pan.
It melted, the white
first clearing to transparent liquid,
then turning solid
and bright again like good laundry.
The yolk kept its yolk shape.
Not fried, not scrambled,
in the end it was cooked.
With pepper and salt, I ate it.
My life that resembled it ate it.
It tasted like any other wrecked thing,
eggish and tender, a banquet.

THREE-LEGGED BLUES

Always you were given
one too many, one too few.
What almost happens, doesn't.
What might be lost, you'll lose.
The crows will eat your garden.
Weeds will get what's left.
Your cats will be three-legged,
your house's mice be blessed.
One friend will take your husband,
another wear your dress.
No, it isn't what you wanted.
It isn't what you'd choose.
Your floors have always slanted.
Your roof has paid its dues.
Life delivered you a present—
a too-small pair of shoes.
What almost happened, won't now.
What can be lost, you'll lose.

A Roomless Door

I walked
past a house

I walked past
a house
I heard weeping

I walked past
my father's
house
I heard weeping

it sounded
like

a piano's 89th key

A Small-Sized Mystery

Leave a door open long enough,
a cat will enter.
Leave food, it will stay.
Soon, on cold nights,
you'll be saying "Excuse me"
if you want to get out of your chair.
But one thing you'll never hear from a cat
is "Excuse me."
Nor Einstein's famous theorem.
Nor "The quality of mercy is not strained."
In the dictionary of Cat, mercy is missing.
In this world where much is missing,
a cat fills only a cat-sized hole.
Yet your whole body turns toward it
again and again because it is there.

BAMBOO

What exists wants to persist.
Even the knock of bamboo on bamboo
spilled outward continues.
And you who have lived—restless, ambitious, aggrieved.
Who have answered to Walter, to Shirley, to Tim,
to Carlos, to Teisha, to Haavo.
Do not think it unchanged, this world you are leaving.

A Day Is Vast

A day is vast.
Until noon.
Then it's over.

Yesterday's pondwater
braided still wet in my hair.

I don't know what time is.

You can't ever find it.
But you can lose it.

A Thought

Some thoughts
throw off
a backward heat
as walls might,
at night, in summer.

It could happen
this moment—

Some movement.

One word's almost
imperceptible shiver.

And what was
long cold
in your left palm,
long cold in your right palm,
might find itself
malleable, warmer.

An apricot
could be planted,
in such a corner.

POMPEII

How many houses
become a living Pompeii,
undusted, unemptied.

Catastrophe is not only sudden.
Hearts stop in more ways than one.

Sometimes the house key is lost,
sometimes the lock.
Sometimes an ending means what did not knock.

ONE LOSS FOLDS ITSELF INSIDE ANOTHER

One loss
folds itself inside another.
It is like the origami
held inside a plain sheet of paper.
Not creased yet.
Not yet more heavy.
The hand stays steady.

STONE AND KNIFE

One angle blunts, another sharpens.
Loss also: stone & knife.

Some griefs augment the heart,
enlarge;
some stunt.

Scentless loosestrife,
rooms unwalked in,
these losses are small.

Others cannot be described at all.

SUITCASE

One ear is going,
packing its suitcase
early.
It is packing the rain.
It is taking some leaves.
These.

Also that russeting bird
in the cloudying
iris,
blurred as a hand
waving goodbye
is.

My Luck

My luck
lay in the road
copper side up
and copper side down
It shone
I passed it by
I turned around
I picked it up
I shook
my beggar's cup
quite full
I left it there
to be refound
I bent down and
I unbent up
copper side down
copper side up
between the air
and ground
left there picked up
My luck

A Hand Is Shaped for
What It Holds or Makes

A hand is shaped for what it holds or makes.
Time takes what's handed to it then—warm bread, a stone,
a child whose fingers touch the page to keep her place.

Beloved, grown old separately, your face
shows me the changes on my own.
I see the histories it holds, the argument it makes

against the thresh of trees, the racing clouds, the race
of birds and sky birds always lose:
       the lines have ranged, but not the cheek's strong bone.
My fingers touching there recall that place.

Once we were one. Then what time did, and hands, erased
us from the future we had owned.
For some, the future holds what hands release, not make.

We made a bridge. We walked it. Laced
night's sounds with passion.
Owls' pennywhistles, after, took our place.

Wasps leave their nest. Wind takes the papery case.
Our wooden house, less easily undone,
now houses others. A life is shaped by what it holds or makes.
I make these words for what they can't replace.

I Ran Out Naked in the Sun

I ran out naked
in the sun
and who could blame me
who could blame

the day was warm

I ran out naked
in the rain
and who could blame me
who could blame

the storm

I leaned toward sixty
that day almost done
it thundered
then

I wanted more I
shouted *More*
and who could blame me
who could blame

had been before

could blame me
that I wanted more

WHEN YOUR LIFE LOOKS BACK

When your life looks back—
as it will, at itself, at you—what will it say?

Inch of colored ribbon cut from the spool.
Flame curl, blue-consuming the log it flares from.
Bay leaf. Oak leaf. Cricket. One among many.

Your life will carry you as it did always,
with ten fingers and both palms,
with horizontal ribs and upright spine,
with its filling and emptying heart,
that wanted only your own heart, emptying, filled, in return.
You gave it. What else could you do?

Immersed in air or in water.
Immersed in hunger or anger.
Curious even when bored.
Longing even when running away.

"What will happen next?"—
the question hinged in your knees, your ankles,
in the in-breaths even of weeping.
Strongest of magnets, the future impartial drew you in.
Whatever direction you turned toward was face to face.
No back of the world existed,
no unseen corner, no test. No other earth to prepare for.

This, your life had said, its only pronoun.
Here, your life had said, its only house.
Let, your life had said, its only order.

And did you have a choice in this? You did—

Sleeping and waking,
the horses around you, the mountains around you,
the buildings with their tall, hydraulic shafts.
Those of your own kind around you—

A few times, you stood on your head.
A few times, you chose not to be frightened.
A few times, you held another beyond any measure.
A few times, you found yourself held beyond any measure.

Mortal, your life will say,
as if tasting something delicious, as if in envy.
Your immortal life will say this, as it is leaving.

THE SUPPLE DEER

The quiet opening
between fence strands
perhaps eighteen inches.

Antlers to hind hooves,
four feet off the ground,
the deer poured through.

No tuft of the coarse white belly hair left behind.

I don't know how a stag turns
into a stream, an arc of water.
I have never felt such accurate envy.

Not of the deer:

To be that porous, to have such largeness pass through me.

ACKNOWLEDGMENTS

All gratitude to the MacDowell Colony, the H. J. Andrews Experimental Forest, the Key West Literary Seminars, and the Vermont Studio Center for residencies and generous hospitality extended during the writing of this book. My thanks also to the magazines and anthologies in which these poems have appeared sometimes in earlier versions or with different titles:

Agenda (U.K.): "Chapel"; *Alaska Quarterly Review:* "Green-Striped Melons"; *The American Poetry Review:* "When Your Life Looks Back," "Izmir," "Stone and Knife," "These Also Once under Moonlight"; *The Atlantic:* "Of Yield and Abandon," "Vinegar and Oil," "The Conversation," "For the *Lobaria, Usnea,* Witches' Hair, Map Lichen, Beard Lichen, Ground Lichen, Shield Lichen"; *The Believer:* "Haofon Rece Swealg"; *Bombay Gin:* "The Dark Hour" (reprint); *The Cortland Review:* "The Egg Had Frozen, an Accident. I Thought of My Life," "Fourth World"; *Drunken Boat:* "China," "Sheep," "Three-Legged Blues"; *Five Points:* "All Day the Difficult Waiting," "The Present," "Protractor," "Rainstorm Visibly Shining in the Left-Out Spoon of a Leaf," "The Tongue Says Loneliness," "Bruises," "Chapel" (reprint), "Contentment," "Suitcase," "Five Pebbles—Like Moonlight Seen in a Well, Glass, Mountain and Mouse, Memorial, Night and Day," "Rain Thinking," "Tolstoy and the Spider," "Red Wine Is Fined by Adding Broken Eggshells" (reprint); *The Georgia Review:* "A Hand Is Shaped for What It Holds or Makes"; *The Great River Review:* "The Egg Had Frozen, an Accident. I Thought of My Life," "Pompeii," "Come, Thief," "A Roomless Door" (all reprints); *Harvard Review:* "First Light Edging Cirrus"; *The Kenyon Review:* "A Day Is Vast," "Sweater," "Two Rains"; *The Manhattan Review:* "Come, Thief," "Haibun: A Mountain Rowboat," "Pompeii," "The Familiar Stairs"; *Marsh Hawk Review:*

"Come, Thief" (reprint); *McSweeney's:* "A Roomless Door," "The Cloudy Vase"; *The New Republic:* "A Small-Sized Mystery"; *The New Yorker:* "French Horn," "If Truth Is the Lure, Humans Are Fishes," "Washing Doorknobs"; *Night Sun:* "Shadow: An Assay"; *Noon* (Japan): "Everything Has Two Endings," "Rainstorm Visibly Shining in the Left-Out Spoon of a Leaf" (both reprints); *Orion:* "Bamboo," "The Supple Deer"; *Ploughshares:* "Critique of Pure Reason"; *Poetry:* "All the Difficult Hours and Minutes," "The Decision," "The Pear," "Seawater Stiffens Cloth," "Perishable, It Said" "Sentencings," "Sonoma Fire"; *Poetry International:* "I Ran Out Naked in the Sun," "It Must Be Leaves," "Love in August," "The Promise"; *Poetry Ireland Review* (Ireland): "China"; and, as reprints, "Critique of Pure Reason," "Rainstorm Visibly Shining in the Left-Out Spoon of a Leaf," "The Lost Love Poems of Sappho"; *Poetry Kanto* (Japan): "Sometimes the Heart Is a Shallow Autumn River"; and, as reprints: "Bamboo," "Shadow: An Assay," "Green-Striped Melons," "A Thought"; *Poetry London* (U.K.): "Everything Has Two Endings," "Sheep," "A Thought"; *Poetry Northwest:* "The Inventive, Visible Hobbles"; *Poetry Review* (U.K.): "The Dark Hour," "Red Wine Is Fined by Adding Broken Eggshells"; *Quarterly West:* "Left-Handed Sugar"; *Slate:* "Invitation," "The Kind Man," "Alzheimer's"; *Spiritus:* "Sometimes the Heart Is a Shallow Autumn River"; *The Threepenny Review:* "Heat and Desperation"; *TLS/Times Literary Supplement* (U.K.): "Narrowness"; *Tin House:* "Hunger," "Wild Plum"; *Tricycle:* "A Blessing for Wedding"; *Vallum* (Canada): "Big-Leaf Maple Standing over Its Own Reflection," "My Luck"; *Water-Stone Review:* "Each We Call Fate," "The Lost Love Poems of Sappho," "The Visible Heat," "The Question," "The Perfection of Loss," "Distance Makes Clean"; *Wild Apples:* "A Thought" (reprint); *Wilderness* (the Wilderness Society newsletter): "Like Moonlight Seen in a Well," "Mountain and Mouse," "Opening the Hands Between Here and Here."

Anthologies: *Best American Poetry 2011:* "The Cloudy Vase"; *Best American Poetry 2007:* "Critique of Pure Reason"; *The Best Spiritual Writing 2010:* "Vinegar and Oil"; *When She Named Fire: An Anthology of Contemporary Poetry by American Women*: "A Hand Is Shaped for What It Holds or Makes," "All Day the Difficult Waiting," "Shadow: An Assay," "Rainstorm Visibly Shining in the Left-Out Spoon of a Leaf," "Critique of Pure Reason," "The Lost Love Poems of Sappho"; *The Way of Natural History:* "The Supple Deer"; *Alhambra Poetry Calendar* (2008, 2009, 2010): "A Blessing for Wedding," "French

Horn," "The Pear"; *Writers on the West:* "Building and Earthquake," "The Dark Hour,"
"The Supple Deer"; *The Autumn House Anthology of Contemporary American Poetry:* "First
Light Edging Cirrus," "The Supple Dear," "Narrowness," "A Hand Is Shaped for
What It Holds or Makes," "Perishable, It Said."

"Pompeii" was commissioned by the composer Evan Chambers for *The Old Bury-
ing Ground* (premiered December 2007, Ann Arbor, Michigan, and February 2008,
Carnegie Hall, New York City). "Opening the Hands between Here and Here" and
"When Your Life Looks Back" were reprinted in *Where the God of Love Hangs Out,* by
Amy Bloom. "Green-Striped Melons" was reprinted in "American Life in Poetry,"
a nationally syndicated newspaper column. "For the *Lobaria, Usnea,* Witches' Hair,
Map Lichen, Beard Lichen, Ground Lichen, Shield Lichen" appeared in a fine press
limited edition broadside to benefit the Association of Literary Scholars, Critics,
and Writers. "Critique of Pure Reason" was distributed worldwide by the *Broad-
sidedpress.org* project. Twelve of these poems appeared in a fine press limited edition
Center for Book Arts chapbook, *The Present.* Eight were first printed as limited edi-
tion letterpress broadsides by the fine printer Jerry Reddan, in his Tangram series.

A NOTE ON THE TYPE

The text of this book was set in Centaur, the only typeface designed by Bruce Rogers (1870–1957), the well-known American book designer. A celebrated penman, Rogers based his design on the roman face cut by Nicolas Jenson in 1470 for his Eusebius. Jenson's roman surpassed all of its forerunners and even today, in modern recuttings, remains one of the most popular and attractive of all typefaces.

The italic used to accompany Centaur is Arrighi, designed by another American, Frederic Warde, and based on the chancery face used by Lodovico degli Arrighi in 1524.

Composed by North Market Street Graphics, Lancaster, Pennsylvania

Printed and bound by Thomson-Shore, Dexter, Michigan

Book design by Robert C. Olsson